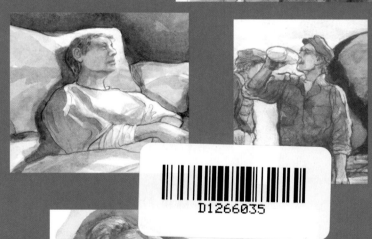

D1266035

Kansas City, MO Public Library
00001840068716

What is a Veteran, Anyway?

Story by Robert C. Snyder, Ph.D.
Illustrations by Ron Himler

 Blue Marlin Publications

What is a Veteran Anyway?

Published by Blue Marlin Publications

Text copyright © 2016 by Robert C. Snyder, Ph.D.
Illustrations copyright © 2016 by Ronald Himler

First printing 2016

Library of Congress Cataloging-in-Publication Data

Names: Snyder, Robert C., 1969- author. | Himler, Ronald, illustrator.
Title: What is a veteran, anyway? / story by Robert C. Snyder, Ph.D.,
  Military Police Captain, US Army Reserve ; illustrations by Ron Himler.
Description: First edition. | West Bay Shore, NY : Blue Marlin Publications,
  Ltd., [2016] | Includes bibliographical references and index. | Audience: Grades K-3.
Identifiers: LCCN 2016018818 | ISBN 9780988529557 (hardcover : alk. paper)
Subjects: LCSH: Veterans--United States--Juvenile literature.
Classification: LCC UB357 .S62 2016 | DDC 305.9/06970973--dc23
LC record available at https://lccn.loc.gov/2016018818

Job #160945

Blue Marlin Publications, Ltd.
823 Aberdeen Road, West Bay Shore, NY 11706
www.bluemarlinpubs.com

Printed and bound by Regent Publishing Services Limited in China.
Book design & layout by Jude Rich

All rights reserved. No part of this publication may be reproduced, stored in or introduced into a retrieval system, or transmitted in any form or by any means (electronic, mechanical, photocopied, recorded or otherwise) without the express written consent of the copyright owners and the publisher of this book.

To the teachers and staff at Dassa McKinney Elementary School, for their unwavering support through personal letters and cards, as well as letters from their students during my deployment to Iraq in 2003. Furthermore, I will never forget how the staff collected money, purchased a Kevlar vest, and sent it to me upon finding out that I was without Army issued body armor on my deployment. Not a morning went by without me gratefully thinking of such wonderful co-workers, as I slipped the vest on to begin my daily mission throughout Baghdad!

- Robert C. Snyder, Ph.D.

To Lt. Col. Eric Himler (Ret) USMC and Family

- Ron Himler

Veterans are special kinds of Americans who answer the call to serve our country when needed.

Veterans may be grandparents, aunts, uncles, cousins, moms, dads, brothers, or sisters to each of us.

A veteran is someone who has served The United States of America in the Army, Air Force, Marines, Navy, Coast Guard, or Merchant Marines.

Veterans work in many different jobs in the military.

Some veterans are police, mechanics, cooks, truck drivers, and construction workers.

Others are pilots, sailors, or foot soldiers called Infantry.

Some parachute from the sky, drive and operate tanks, or set up artillery cannons.

Veterans might be recent high school graduates.

They also might be lawyers, doctors, and teachers.

Some veterans have trained and prepared for war without ever needing to defend America from far away.

But other veterans have served America during times of war. Whenever necessary, veterans fight in wars against people who wish harm to Americans or other innocent people.

Veterans sacrifice time with their families in order to travel far away to protect Americans from people who do not like our freedom.

Veterans endure many hardships. Often, they live in tents in remote woodland areas or open deserts.

They sometimes give up the comforts of home such as running water, hot food, a bed, and even just a warm, dry place to sleep.

Instead, veterans get water from a water buffalo, which is a water tank on wheels.

They often eat food sealed in a plastic pouch called a field ration or Meal, Ready-to-Eat (MRE). This food tastes kind of like a cafeteria lunch, but is usually eaten cold from the pouch instead of hot on a plate.

Sometimes veterans have to sleep on the ground wrapped in only rain ponchos. Other times, they sleep huddled together to protect themselves from cold or harsh weather.

Veterans sometimes endure rough weather, such as 140-degree desert heat or -10-degree cold in frigid mountains. Imagine having to sleep outside in the snow after spending time playing outside, when you just want go inside to get warm. Or imagine lying down on desert sand that is as hot as beach sand that burns your feet as you run for the relief of the cool water!

Veterans do their jobs even when faced with clouds of dust or pouring rain.

Veterans withstand all kinds of pests, such as mosquitoes, ticks, sand fleas, scorpions, mice, and even rats.

Veterans give up sleep to work long nights on guard duty.

Veterans battle diseases such as pneumonia, diarrhea, and infected cuts.

Sometimes, veterans may be forced to go days or weeks without a shower.

It may be even longer without a change of clothes.

Showers sometimes come from a jug or bucket. Veterans might use these to wash their bodies and clothing.

When it is dark, a veteran's only light may come from a flashlight because there may not be any electricity.

Veterans spend a lot of time in groups, making new friends with each other because they are far away from loved ones.

But sometimes, veterans have nobody and nothing but the lonely ground below and the night sky above.

Unfortunately, some veterans have sacrificed much more than sleep, showers, and the comforts of home. These veterans have suffered terrible wounds from bullets, bombs or bayonets, which are like long knives that connect to the tip of a soldier's rifle.

Some veterans have even sacrificed their lives to protect the freedom we have.

So, why do veterans volunteer to endure these dangers and hardships?

Simply put, veterans want to preserve, defend, and protect the precious freedom that everyone in America loves and needs.

Sometimes, the only way to do that is for some Americans to fight for our country so that all Americans can stay safe. Even with the fear and danger of injury or death, these special Americans proudly defend our country and our freedom.

American Veterans have served in many wars, including the American Revolutionary War, War of 1812, Mexican War, Civil War, Indian Wars, War with Spain, China Relief Expedition, Philippine Insurrection, Mexican Expedition, World War I, World War II, Korean War, Vietnam War, and Persian Gulf War.

They have also served in wars in places such as the Dominican Republic, Iran, Lebanon, Grenada, Panama, Somalia, Haiti, Kosovo, Afghanistan, and Iraq.

To honor all these brave men and women who have served America, we have a holiday every November 11th called Veterans Day.

Veterans Day is not a holiday for opening presents, eating candy, or watching fireworks, but there is one very special thing that everyone can do. That special thing we can all do on this holiday—or any day of the year—is say **Thank You** to a veteran!

Here are some ways YOU can thank a veteran any day of the year, even today!

- Make a card for a veteran in your local nursing home or veterans hospital.
- Visit a veteran in your local nursing home or veterans hospital.
- With approval from your teacher, invite a veteran to speak to your class at your school.
- Interview a veteran, and record your interview for your school or local newspaper.
- Send a letter and/or care package to a veteran who is sacrificing time away from family.
    * If you don't have any money to purchase items for a care package, consider giving away some of your own candy this Halloween! Here are some great organizations to help you get your letters or packages to the soldiers:
        - www.amillionthanks.org
        - www.operationgratitude.com
        - www.forthetroops.org

- Participate in a parade to support and thank veterans. Some really great organizations that support veterans through parades include:
    * The Wounded Warrior Project - www.woundedwarriorproject.org
    * The Tunnel to Towers Foundation—helps to build homes for catastrophically injured veterans - www.tunnel2towers.org
    * Hope for The Warriors - www.hopeforthewarriors.org
    * United Services Organization (USO) - www.uso.org

- Participate in a walk, run, bike ride, or other fund raiser for veterans.
- Organize a fund raiser (e.g., lemonade stand, candy sale, cupcake drive) to raise awareness and money for your favorite veterans charitable organization.